Margaret Mahy is a New Zealander and has loved
thinking up stories ever since she was a small girl.
She has been awarded the highly acclaimed Carnegie
Medal twice (for *The Haunting* – published in 1982,
and *The Changeover* – 1984) and the Esther Glen
Award three times. She lives near Christchurch,
South Island in a house she partially built herself.
Margaret has two grown-up daughters, several cats
and an enormous number of books.

Wonderful Me!

Margaret Mahy

Illustrated by Peter Bailey

Dolphin Paperbacks

Contents

Teddy and the Witches

Once there were three witches flying over the world and looking down at it from their broomsticks. One had white hair, one had black hair, and one had hair like wild bright flame, and all three had gleaming golden eyes . . . They were looking for mischief to do.

At last they came to a long, green valley which they had never seen before in all their magic lives, and their eyes shone as they looked at the snug-as-a-bug-in-a-rug farms and the soft, smudgy shadows in the creases of the hills.

'Here,' they said to each other, 'is a wonderful place for some mischief.' And they smiled . . .

The first witch pointed her finger. *Tweedle dee!* All the pigs grew silver wings and flew up into the trees with the magpies.

The second witch clapped her hands and all the hens turned into parrots and cockatoos - scarlet and green, white and yellow - and filled the air with their merry screechings.

But the third witch, the redheaded one, just blinked her golden eyes and all the cows became elephants - and elephants eat a lot of grass and are very hard to milk.

Then the witches sat back to enjoy the mischief, like wasps round a honey pot.

Now, in this valley lived a small boy called Teddy. He had brown eyes, he was always hungry, and his head was full of deep, secret ways of thinking. And when he went out the next morning and found

2

the hen run full of parrots and cockatoos he
thought to himself, 'Witches!' And when he
saw Next-Door-Farmer's fields full of large
grey crumpled-looking elephants he
thought to himself, 'Witches!' And then
when he heard the pigs squealing in the
trees, he thought, 'It's those witches again. I
must do something about them.'

And so Teddy sat down with a ball of
string and some ends of rope and worked at

a secret thing. His mother walked by him to the clothesline.

'What are you making, little Teddy?' she asked. 'Is it a net of some kind?'

'It isn't a net,' Teddy answered. 'It's called "Little Hand Snatching at the Stars".'

His mother smiled and went on her way. She did not know that 'Little Hand Snatching at the Stars' was part of a witch trap.

It was late in the afternoon when the witch trap was finished. Teddy hung it between two tall pine trees, and on the ground underneath the trap he put some pieces of a broken mirror, two shining tin lids and some teaspoons which he had taken from the drawer when his mother wasn't looking. The idea was that the witches would see these bright things shining and would fly down to see what they were. And then they would be caught in the trap . . .

Sure enough, next morning when Teddy looked out of the window, he saw something like a flame caught beneath the pine trees. There, very beautiful and glowing, was the youngest witch – the redheaded one – like a fly in a spider's web. Down on the ground lay her pointed hat, her cloak and broomstick.

Teddy ran out into the garden.

'Hello little fellow,' she said very sweetly to Teddy. 'Could you pass me my broomstick and hat please?'

Teddy knew that a witch's magic lies in her hat and broomstick. He did not give them to her, but took them inside and hid them in his wardrobe behind the raincoats. Then he took a skipping-rope, and went out to the witch again. After he had set her free from the witch trap, Teddy tied the skipping-rope round her ankles.

'What are you going to do with me?' she asked, so sweetly that it was hard to believe she would do any mischief. But in the next paddock Teddy could see great bare patches eaten by elephants that had once been cows.

'During the day,' he said, 'you will be able to help my mother. But at night I will tie you up to the hen house. If it rains you can get inside.' (This was not at all cruel as witches are used to perching at night.)

'But I don't like parrots,' said the witch, looking at the gaily-coloured hen run.

'You should have thought of that before,' Teddy answered.

'Well, I won't be here long anyway,' said the witch, with a toss of her wild red hair. 'My sisters will set me free very quickly and you will be sorry you ever thought of making a witch trap.'

Teddy's mother was surprised when he brought the witch inside, but she listened to his story and said that the witch might dry the breakfast dishes. At first the witch was sulky and cross, but as the morning passed she grew more cheerful. Then, just before lunch, the delivery man's van drove up and the young driver got out to bring in the box of groceries that Teddy's mother had ordered.

It was plain the witch was very pleased with his black curly hair and merry eyes.

'Is he a prince?' she asked Teddy.

'No, he's the delivery man,' Teddy answered.

'How are you, fellow,' the delivery man said to Teddy as he came in. He looked at the witch. It was plain he was very pleased with her wild red hair and golden eyes. After he had talked for a while he went off - leaving a dozen eggs that should have gone to somebody else. After this the witch seemed almost happy.

Before he went to bed that night Teddy pinned a spray of fern to his pyjamas. He had read somewhere that it was a good protection against witch spells. It was just

as well he did, for in the night there was
more witch trouble . . .

Teddy had fallen asleep when, suddenly,
his bed shook itself and then flew out of
the window. Outside, the two witches
screamed at him.

'Give us back our sister,' they screeched.
They flew at him, making claws with their
long fingers. 'Give us back our sister or you
will go for a wild ride.'

Teddy was not afraid. He answered, 'First you must take the magic off the valley and give us back our cows and hens.'

'Never, never!' yelled the witches. They tried to magic Teddy, but the spells bounced back with a twanging sound. This was because of the fern Teddy was wearing.

'Well,' said the white-haired witch, 'we may not be able to touch you, but we can change your bed.'

Then Teddy's bed began to buck and kick, to slide and glide, to bumble and stumble, to creep and leap, and to highstep and lowstep, until Teddy felt quite giddy.

'Will you set her free?' the witches screamed. (They could not rescue her themselves without her broomstick and hat and cloak, and of course they did not know where Teddy had hidden them.)

'Of course I won't,' Teddy answered.

Then his bed became a wild horse, with

furious wings and hoofs of thunder, and it raced wildly up and down the valley. But Teddy held on tightly with his knees, and twisted his hands in its mane – and after a while the horse stood still.

Then the bed became a fiery dragon which hissed and twisted to get at Teddy, but he curled up small between the dragon's wings, and it could not get him. And so, in its turn, the dragon grew still.

And then the bed became a great wind and it tossed Teddy about, but he lay limp in the wind and thought happy thoughts, and pretended he was being bounced in his bed at home.

At last the white-haired witch said, 'That was just my sister's magic. I'm going to send you round the world!' She said something to the bed which at once set off at a terrific speed and flew all the way round the world. But Teddy sat in the middle of his bed and sang nursery rhymes and took no notice at all of the hot or the cold, or the green or the gold, or the pounding, bounding sea. At last the bed came home again, and as it did so, there was the sound of breaking violin strings. The witches had taken their spells off the valley. Down from the trees floated the pigs. The silver wings shook themselves free and fluttered off to another place. Where they went I can't tell you at all. And the parrots and cockatoos – scarlet and green, white and yellow – became clucking, scratching hens again.

Then the oldest witch – the white-haired one – said to Teddy, 'The mischief is undone, as far as we can undo it. Our sister must undo her own spell, and turn the elephants back to cows.' Then they flew away into the new morning that was poking its bright face over the hills.

When he got up, Teddy went into the kitchen. The witch was putting apples on the stove to stew for breakfast. She wore one of his mother's aprons, and her long red hair hung in a pigtail down her back.

'Your sisters have taken off their magic,' Teddy told her. 'And if you turn the elephants back to cows I will give you back your broomstick, cloak and hat.'

'My sisters?' said the witch. 'My broomstick? Oh yes, that's right. I'm a witch! I had forgotten.' She waved her hand and there was the sound of a bell note, faint, far away and rather sad. 'There now, the magic is gone.'

'Well, thank you,' Teddy answered. 'I'll go and get your broomstick.'

'Keep it yourself,' said the witch. 'I don't want it. I like it here. I'm tired of being a witch. Besides, tonight I'm going to the cinema with the delivery man.'

'Really, I can't think what I'd do without her,' said Teddy's mother. 'She is such a help to me. It's just like magic.'

The witch looked pleased.

Teddy thought for a while. 'Can I really

have your hat and broomstick?' he asked, at last.

'You might as well,' she answered, 'for I don't want them.'

The people in the valley had just got over their surprise at finding their pigs, hens and cows had come back to them, when they were surprised again to see Teddy on a broomstick and wearing a high steeple hat, flying overhead.

'There's that Teddy!' they said to each other. 'What will he be up to next?'

The broomstick flicked a bit as if it were laughing. But Teddy pointed upwards, and it flew higher and higher, like a little bird trying to reach the sun. Up into the blue, blue air it went, and there Teddy soared and swooped like a small wind, happy among the clouds.

Gay Wind

A gay wind, merry with autumn,
Comes round the chimney stack
Carrying bright leaf riders
High on its bounding back.

And the chimney standing stiffly,
So brave and black and bold,
Looks like a strong stern soldier
Hung with medals of gold.

And the chimney standing stiffly,
Where mortar and brick have bound him,
Looks like a dark enchanter
With dancers of gold around him.

The Playground

Just where the river curled out to meet the sea was the town playground, and next to the playground in a tall cream-coloured house lived Linnet. Every day after school she stood for a while at her window watching the children over the fence, and longing to run out and join them. She could hear the squeak squeak of the swings going up and down, up and down all afternoon. She could see children bending their knees pushing themselves up into the sky. She would think to herself, 'Yes, I'll go down now. I won't stop to think about it. I'll run out and have a turn on the slide,' but then she would feel her hands getting hot and her stomach shivery, and she knew she was frightened again.

Jim her brother and Alison her sister (who was a year younger than Linnet) were not frightened of the playground. Alison could fly down the slide with her arms held wide, chuckling as she went. Jim would spin on the roundabout until he felt more like a top than a boy, then he would jump off and roll over in the grass shouting with laughter. But when Linnet went on the slide the smooth shiny wood burned the backs of her legs, and she shot off the end so fast she tumbled over and made all the other children laugh. When she went on the roundabout the trees and the sky smudged into one another and she felt sick. Even the swings frightened her and she held their chains so tightly that the links left red marks in her hands.

'Why should I be so scared?' she wondered. 'If only I could get onto the swing and swing without thinking about it I'd be all right. Only babies fall off. I wouldn't mind being frightened of lions or wolves but it is terrible to be frightened of swings and seesaws.'

Then a strange thing happened. Linnet's mother forgot to pull the blind down one night. The window was open and a little wind came in smelling of the ropes and tar on the wharf and of the salt sea beyond. Linnet sighed in her sleep and turned over. Then the moon began to set lower in the sky. It found her window and looked in at her. Linnet woke up.

The moonlight made everything quite different and enchanted. The river was pale and smooth and its other bank, the sandspit around which it twisted to find the sea, was absolutely black. The playground which was so noisy and crowded by day was deserted. It looked strange because it was so

still and because the red roundabout, the
green slide, and the blue swings were all
grey in the moonlight. It looked like the
ghost of a playground, or a faded
clockwork toy waiting for daylight, and
happy children to wind it up and set it
going again. Linnet heard the town clock
strike faintly. Midnight. She thought some of
the moon silver must have got into the
clock's works because it sounded softer, yet

clearer than it did during the day. As she
thought this she was startled to see shadows
flicker over the face of the moon. 'Witches?'
she wondered before she had time to tell
herself that witches were only make
believe people. Of course it wasn't witches.
It was a flock of birds flying inland from
the sea.

'They're going to land on the river bank,'
she thought. 'How funny, I didn't know
birds could fly at night. I suppose it is
because it is such bright moonlight.'

They landed and were lost to sight in a
moment, but just as she began to look
somewhere else a new movement caught
her eye and she looked back again. Out
from under the trees fringing the riverbank,
from the very place where the birds had
landed, came children running, bouncing
and tumbling: their voices and laughter
came to her, faint as chiming bells.

Linnet could see their bare feet shaking

and crushing the grass, their wild floating
hair, and even their mischievous shining
eyes. They swarmed all over the
playground. The swings began to swing, the
seesaws started their up and down, the
roundabout began to spin. The children
laughed and played while Linnet watched
them, longing more than ever before to run
out and join in the fun. It wasn't that she
was afraid of the playground this time - it

was just that she was shy. So she had to be content to stare while all the time the swings swept back and forth loaded with the midnight children, and still more children crowded the roundabout, the seesaw and the bars.

How long she watched Linnet could not say. She fell asleep watching, and woke up with her cheek on the windowsill. The morning playground was quite empty and was bright in its daytime colours once more.

'Was it all dreams?' wondered Linnet blinking over breakfast. 'Will they come again tonight?'

'Wake up, stupid,' Alison called. 'It's time to be off. We'll be late for school.'

All day Linnet wondered about the playground and the children playing there by moonlight. She seemed slower and quieter than ever. Jim and Alison teased her, calling her Old Dreamy, but Linnet did not tell them what dreams she had.

That night the moon woke Linnet once more and she sat up in a flash, peering out anxiously to see if the midnight children were there. The playground, colourless and strange in its nightdress, was empty, but within a minute Linnet heard the beat of wings in the night. Yes, there were the birds coming in from the sea, landing under the trees and, almost at once, there were the children, moonlit and laughing, running to the playground for their night games. Linnet leaned farther out of her window to watch them, and one of them suddenly saw her and pointed at her. All the children came and stood staring over the fence at her. For a few seconds they just stayed like that, Linnet peering out at them and the midnight children, moon-silver and smiling, looking back at her. Their hair, blown behind them by the wind, was as pale as sea foam. Their eyes were as dark and deep as sea caves and shone like stars.

Then the children began to beckon and wave and jump up and down with their arms half out to her, they began to skip and dance with delight. Linnet slid out of bed, climbed out of the window and over the fence all in her nightgown. The midnight children crowded up to her, caught her and whirled her away.

Linnet thought it was like dancing some strange dance. At one moment she was on the roundabout going round and round and giggling with the other children at the prickly dizzy feeling it gave her, in the next she was sweeping in a follow-my-leader down the slide. Then someone took her hand and she was on the seesaw with a child before her and a child behind and three more on the other end.

Up went the seesaw.

'Oh, I'm flying!' cried Linnet. Down went the seesaw. Bump went Linnet, and she laughed at the unexpected bouncy jolt when the seesaw end hit the rubber tyre beneath it. Then she was on the swing. She had never been so high before. It seemed to Linnet that at any moment the swing was going to break free and fly off on its own, maybe to the land where the midnight children came from. The swing felt like a great black horse plunging through the night, like a tall ship tossing over the green waves.

'Oh,' cried Linnet, 'it's like having wings.' The children laughed with her, waved and smiled, and they swept around in their playground dance, but they didn't speak. Sometimes she heard them singing, but they were always too far away for her to hear the words.

When, suddenly, the midnight children left their games and started to run for the shadow of the trees, Linnet knew that for tonight at least she must go home as well, but she was too excited to feel sad. As she climbed through the window again she heard the beat of wings in the air and saw the birds flying back to the sea. She waved to them, but in the next moment they were quite gone, and she and the playground were alone again.

Next day when Alison and Jim set out for the playground Linnet said she was coming too. 'Don't come to me if you fall off anything,' said Jim scornfully.

Alison was kinder. 'I'll help you on the roundabout,' she said. 'You hang on to me if you feel giddy.'

'But I won't feel giddy!' Linnet said, and Alison stared at her, surprised to hear her so confident and happy. However, this was just the beginning of the surprises for Alison and Jim. Linnet went on the roundabout and sat there without hanging on at all. On the swing she went almost as high as the boys, and she sat on the seesaw with her arms folded.

'Gosh, Linnet's getting brave as anything over at the playground,' said Jim at tea that night.

'I always knew she had it in her,' said Daddy.

The next night, and the next, Linnet climbed out of her window and joined the beckoning children in the silver playground. During the day, these midnight hours seemed like enchanted dreams and not very real. All the same Linnet was happy and excited knowing she had a special secret all to herself. Her eyes sparkled, she laughed a lot, and got braver and braver in the playground until all the children stopped what they were doing to watch her.

'Gee, Mum,' Alison said, 'you should see Linnet. She goes higher on the swing than any of the boys – much higher than Jim. Right up almost over the top.'

'I hope you're careful, dear,' her mother said.

'I'm all right,' Linnet cried. 'I'm not the least bit scared.'

'Linnet used to be frightened as anything,' Alison said, 'but now she's braver than anybody else.'

Linnet's heart swelled with pride. She could hardly wait until the moon and the tide brought her wonderful laughing night-time companions. She wanted them to admire her and gasp at her as the other children did. They came as they had on other nights, and she scrambled over the fence to join them.

'Look at me!' she shouted, standing on the end of the seesaw and going up and down. The child on the other end laughed and stood up too, but on its hands, not on its feet. It stayed there not over-balancing at all. Linnet slid away as soon as she could and ran over to the swings. She worked herself up higher and higher until she thought she was lost among the stars far far above the playground and the world, all on her own.

'Look at me,' she called again. 'Look at me.'

But the child on the next swing smiled over its shoulder and went higher – just a little higher. Then Linnet lost her temper.

'It's cleverer for me,' she shouted, 'because I'm a real live child, but you – you're only a flock of birds.'

Suddenly silence fell, the laughter died away, the singers stopped their songs. The swings swung lower, the roundabout turned slower, the seesaws stopped for a moment. Linnet saw all the children's pale faces turn towards her: then, without a sound, they began to run back to the shadow of the trees. Linnet felt cold with sadness. 'Don't go,' she called. 'Please don't go.' They did not seem to hear her.

'I'm sorry I said it,' she cried after them, her voice sounding very small and thin in the moonlit silent playground. 'I didn't mean it.' But no – they would not stop even though she pleaded, 'Don't go!' yet again. The playground was empty already and she knew she couldn't follow her midnight children. For the last time she spoke to them.

'I'm sorry!' she whispered and, although it was only a whisper, they must have heard because they answered her. Their voices and laughter drifted back happy and friendly saying their own goodbye. The next moment she saw for the last time the bird flying over the sea to the secret land they came from. Linnet stood alone and barefooted in the playground, the wind pulling at her nightgown. How still and empty it was now. She pushed at a swing and it moved giving a sad little squeak that echoed all round. There was nothing for Linnet to do but go back to bed.

She was never afraid of the playground again and had lots and lots of happy days there laughing and chattering with her friends. Yet sometimes at night, when the moon rose and looked in at her window, she would wake up and look out at the playground just in case she should see the moon and the tide bringing her a flock of strange night-flying birds, which would turn into children and call her out to play with them. But the playground was always empty, the shining midnight children, with their songs and laughter, were gone forever.

Welcoming Song

Dance upon silver, dance upon gold,
We have a baby, one day old.

Dance on a peacock, dance on a pearl,
The baby's a sister, because it's a girl.

Dance upon velvet, dance upon silk,
It sleeps in its cradle and dreams about
 milk.

Dance upon butterflies, dance upon bells,
Its little curled hands are like little pink
 shells.

'Its name?' the wind asks in a whispery
   tongue.
But its name is a secret too dear to be sung.

The Little Boy Who Wanted a Flat World

There was once this little boy sitting in the back of a class at school, listening to a teacher. The teacher had a globe of the world on her desk and was talking to the children about it.

'Once upon a time,' she said, 'people thought the world was flat, but now we know it is round, just like the globe here.'

The little boy looked at the globe, but he wasn't at all pleased with it. In his mind he imagined the world as quite flat, with all the seas pouring over the edge of it, down and down, smooth as glass, down through space, rustling between the stars. He liked the idea of a flat world so much better than a round one, just as he liked glass castles and unicorns and mermaids singing.

'All nice things are pretendings,' he thought. 'None of them are real.' And he went on feeling sorry that the world was round all day.

He was a very little boy you see.

That very night the little boy woke up, feeling the dark grow suddenly warm around him. He found he was lying in long grass in the sunshine. He was not as surprised as you might think, though he was rather dismayed to find himself in such bright clothes . . . and not in ordinary clothes at that. He seemed to be wearing a short skirt and long stockings, and his hair was long too. Then, along came a group of other children and he saw that the boys

were dressed just as he was, and the little
girls wore dresses down to their ankles.

'Well,' he thought, 'I have got myself into a
long-ago time when people dressed
differently.' He didn't bother about his
clothes any more, but felt happy again. He
joined in with them, and off they went
down a stony, bumpy street chasing
pigeons and talking away to each other.

As they went on their noisy, chattering

way they came upon a tall, lean man by the roadside, sitting with his chin on his knees.

'Look, it's Wilkin,' the children cried, crowding around him. 'Tell us a story, Wilkin! Sing us a song!'

Wilkin had a torn blue cloak and a blue tunic. His solemn dark face suddenly broke into smiles. He put his arm around the youngest child and he sang.

'I woke in the morning and looked at the day.
I saw it was asking that I should be gay
So dancing I went with a leap and a bound,
And a song as glad as the world is round.'

'But the world isn't really round, silly Wilkin!' said a little child. 'It's as flat as a penny, and the sea falls over the edge.'

So then the little boy knew that somehow he had woken up in that long time ago when the world was flat.

'But last night,' Wilkin told the children, 'I had a dream. I dreamed I was out in the sky - far, far, far out, where the stars hold their small bright lamps. And do you know what - I could see our world, and it was quite round. Round like a little shining jewel, a spark of glowing fire. When I flew closer I could see the blue sea on it, and the lands like green and brown patches. I saw these things through the streaks of drifting cloud.

Yes, and I could see day and night chasing each other round the world, and ships sailing and sailing and coming back to where they started, and I thought what a beautiful world it was, and how wonderful it would be if it were really round. Why, just think – I could start off from here and run like lightning, leap from wave to wave, step over forests and lakes and mountains, and be back here again before you could wink. But with a flat world I'd just fall over the edge.'

Then all the children laughed.

'No one can run from land to land,' said one, 'and anyway the world is flat.'

'There is no other country over the sea,' said one, 'but only strange monsters that will eat you, Wilkin.'

'The world is flat, Wilkin,' cried a third.

'The world is flat,' Wilkin repeated sadly. 'And all poetry is dust.' The little boy saw that Wilkin was disappointed at seeing his bright dreams burst like bubbles on the children's pinprick words, so he moved closer to Wilkin and pulled his sleeve.

'Really, the world is round,' he whispered, and he and Wilkin smiled a secret smile at each other.

At that moment far away the little boy heard someone call his name. He turned to look over his shoulder, and saw the wallpaper of his own room. He had been in bed dreaming.

Later, as the little boy ate his breakfast, he asked his mother, 'Which is it most beautiful for worlds to be . . . flat or round?'

'It depends,' his mother answered, 'on what you think yourself.'

'I think round worlds are quite nice after all,' the little boy said thoughtfully. He smiled to himself and went on eating his breakfast.

Wonderful Me!

On one side the hills
On the other the sea,
On the beach in the middle
There's wonderful me.

I am made out of sticks
I am made out of salt,
And whatever might happen
It isn't my fault.

I am made out of seaweed
I'm made out of stones,
And my heart is a bird
In a cage of white bones.

I am made out of froth
I am made out of foam,
I am spinning the world
So I daren't go home,

Or else like a penny,
Or else like a top,
The world would spin slower,
     and slower
   and stop.

On the beach in the middle
There's wonderful me,
And on one side the hills,
On the other the sea.

Right-Hand Men

There was once a boy called Jack who was too small to go to school and too old to play with his baby sister. The trouble was that there were no other children for Jack to play with – not for miles – and he was often quite lonely. There was plenty to do on the farm where he lived, but the happiest part of doing things is sharing them with somebody else, and that is just what Jack missed most.

Sometimes he would go and talk with an old man who lived in a hut on a hill. Funnily enough the old man's name was Jack too, so there were a pair of them – Old

Jack and Little Jack - talking together on the hillside. Old Jack told Little Jack stories of England where he had been born and of Australia and South America where he had lived for many years. This was often interesting and exciting, but it was only talking after all. You couldn't expect an Old Jack to go exploring the creek, or to go swinging out over the water on a creeper and falling in with a splash, or even to go climbing trees. He just sat and talked, screwing his eyes up at the sky, squinting at the clouds. Sometimes Little Jack felt Old Jack had forgotten all about him, and was just talking to the world.

One day Little Jack asked Old Jack a question.

'Did you have boys to play with when you were small, Jack?'

And then Old Jack turned his eyes away from the sky and looked at him thoughtfully.

'Why – yes! I had five!' he said at last.

'What were their names?' asked Little Jack, because he liked to hear about other boys.

'They were the most curious set of boys I ever came across,' said Old Jack, 'and these were their names – Tommy Thumbkin, Billie Winkie, Long Duster, Jacky Molebar and Little Perky.'

Little Jack's mouth and eyes grew as round as rabbit holes.

'What names!' he cried, and he said them over and over with Old Jack correcting him until he knew them by heart.

'They had lots of names,' said Old Jack. 'Other places call them by different ones, according to what place it is, but this is what we called them in Cheshire, where I was born.'

'What were they like?' asked Little Jack. 'How old were they?'

'As to age I couldn't rightly say,' said Old Jack. 'Though mostly they were my age and not a moment more or less – they were what you might call my right-hand men. Tommy Thumbkin – he was a short serious sort of boy, brave as a lion mind you, but a bit different from the others who were great ones for laughing. He used to whistle sweet as thrushes and blackbirds did Tommy, and wander off a bit on his own.

'Billie Winkie was a sailor boy – one of

the old-fashioned sort that wore pigtails. He was strong and brown and had a funny rolling walk as if all the world was a ship deck. Long Duster - now he was a funny one - t-a-l-l,' said Old Jack stretching the word out.

'T-a-l-l and gentle with long hair and a sad face. Even his laughing had something sad in it - mind you, he wasn't sad company at all. He was great on the tree climbing because he had two great long arms on him. Jack Molebar - you'd have looked twice at him before you realized he was a boy because he was covered in black fur like a pussycat, only his face looking out, and a white tuft under his chin. Everything made him laugh - he was a really merry one.

'And as for Little Perky - he was a biscuit-coloured boy with foxy red hair, but the strangest things about him were his pricked-up ears, sharp like a smart little dog's always listening for the joke, and also his waving plumy tail.'

'Tail!' said Little Jack. But Old Jack fell silent. 'Gosh,' said Little Jack, 'I wish I'd known those boys.'

'Well, so you do,' Old Jack replied, 'for they're friends to every Jack that's born into this world with a thumb and four fingers. Look —' He took Little Jack's hand and said their names over slowly. 'Tommy Thumbkin (that's your thumb), Billie Winkie (that's your first beckoning finger, you see). Long Duster (he's the longest finger you understand). Jacky Molebar (there's Jacky), and Little Perky (he's the smallest). Now when you see your right hand, for work or play you've got five fine friends to keep you company.'

When Little Jack went off down the hill on the way home, he found he was not gone very far before someone put a furry

paw into his hand and when he looked to
the left – there was Jacky Molebar, and
someone thumped him on the shoulder and
there was Billie Winkie with sailor's earrings
golden in his ears. Tall and slender and
smiling shyly Long Duster looked down at
him, and at his heels Little Perky laughed
and danced and pulled funny foxy faces.
And some distance away whistling shrill
and sweet, Tommy Thumbkin nodded to
him and waved a hand.

'You're real!' cried Little Jack. 'You're not
just pretending!'

'Oh, we're real all right,' said Billie Winkie.
'You just haven't been able to see us
before because you didn't know we were
here.'

'But we were!' cried Jacky Molebar. 'We
were here all the time,' and he laughed and
turned head over heels so that dead leaves
stuck to his black fur.

'You're covered in leafmould, mouldy old

Jacky Molebar,' screamed Little Perky, showing off, and he began a strange comical dance pulling such odd faces that they all laughed.

'We'll have lots of fun,' murmured Tommy Thumbkin quietly. 'The good times are coming.'

But Long Duster looked at Little Jack and said, 'I'm not surprised you didn't know

whether we were real or not. I'm not quite sure myself.'

'That's why he's so sad,' Billie Winkie said, 'but – why, I don't know anyone realler than we are – most people aren't half as real. And now for adventure.'

What adventures they had that long golden summer. Little Jack didn't have time to stop and wonder whether or not his funny friends were real or just dreams. When they went exploring down the creek they found magical seas with islands in them. They were shipwrecked lots of times and once they were captured by pirates. Fortunately Tommy Thumbkin got free and helped them escape. They fought the pirates with swords, drove them off their ship onto an island and left them there. Billie Winkie sailed the pirate ship round all the islands and they found enough treasure and parrots and monkeys for them all to have some. They hunted lions in the jungle, fought great battles with bloodthirsty enemies, built castles as high as clouds, and rescued each other from all sorts of great dangers. Things were quite different for Little Jack when Tommy Thumbkin, Billie Winkie, Long Duster, Jacky Molebar and Little Perky went adventuring with him.

Then one day Jack's mother told him his cousin Alan was coming to stay. Jack told his five friends and they were all very excited though Long Duster seemed a little uncertain.

'There's those that don't like us,' he said. 'Suppose your cousin Alan is one of them.'

'Of course he'll like us,' squeaked Little Perky. 'Aren't we the finest set of fellows we know? He'll love us.'

When Alan came he turned out to be an ordinary boy, very friendly and pleased with the country, and slightly older than Jack. He was five years old and going to school. There was never a boy browner or sturdier than Alan. Somehow he was very real.

The strange thing was that he did not seem to see Jack's five funny friends or take any sort of notice of them at first. He listened to Jack talk about them and talk to them, with a puzzled face, sometimes a scornful face, as if he didn't understand all that was going on and did not like what he did understand. Then suddenly he said:

'I can see them now, those boys you're talking to Jack, those right-hand men.' Jack saw Alan smile in a grown-up way as he said this, and he looked quickly at his right-hand men to see if they were at all worried by the smile. It struck him that they looked somehow dim and far away, almost as if their colours had been washed out. They smiled and nodded to him, but Long Duster's smile was very sad and for a moment Jack felt sad too. Then Alan said:

'Come on – let's play down in the creek,' and off they all went, hunting a fierce rare animal with a horse's body and a lion's head and a snake's tail. They tracked it for miles – or so it seemed to Jack – and then came the catching of it. Alan wanted to gallop after it on horses and lassoo it, but Jacky Molebar wanted to dig a pit with nets of flax at the bottom and then chase the animal into the pit. Jack explained to Alan and then Alan said a funny thing.

'Yes, but we don't have to do what he says, do we? He isn't real. He's just pretending isn't he?'

Jack stood still and behind him he felt the right-hand men waiting and listening and watching him hard. In front of him Alan watched and waited too, brown and real – really real.

'Isn't he?' Alan said again. 'You know he's just made up.'

'Yes – I s'pose he is,' Jack said slowly. 'They're all just a game really.'

He blinked his eyes and looked around. Where was furry Jacky Molebar now? Where were Tommy Thumbkin, Billie Winkie and foxy Little Perky? They were all gone. Only Long Duster lingered for a moment still smiling sadly at Jack.

'You see?' he said. 'I thought we weren't real.' And he waved his thin hand and went out like a light. Jack stood staring after him.

'Come on!' Alan said impatiently. 'I'll tell you what, though! We'll leave them here to look after the camp and you and me'll ride after that animal and catch it by ourselves with our lassoos. Say those others sleep in and don't come with us.'

'All right then,' said Jack because there was nothing else to say, and off he went with Alan galloping after the strange animal.

Alan stayed all the Christmas holidays, and then in February Jack was five and went to school. So he wasn't ever lonely again, and didn't really have time to wonder what had become of his right-hand men until one Saturday, a long long time later, he told Old Jack all about it. Old Jack nodded slowly.

'Just the same with me,' he grumbled. 'They off and left me when I made other friends. That's the way with the right-hand men.'

'Where have they gone?' asked Little Jack.

'Off to find some other Jack – a Jack-be-nimble or a Jack-o'dandy – it doesn't matter which –' said Old Jack '– but a lonely Jack somewhere's needing friends. They'll be climbing trees this minute or building forts in the bracken, or maybe digging for treasure. Who can say?'

And he screwed up his eyes at the blue sky, and waved his hand to the sun so that the long shadows of his five fingers danced over the bright grass.

When I Was
But a Little Boy

When I was but a little boy and played
   beneath a tree,
Seven kings and seven queens there came
   to talk with me.
Their hair was blue as lightning beneath
   their crowns of gold,
Their faces all were fair and young - their
   shining eyes were old.
One wore the moon upon his breast,
   another wore the sun,
The others wore the frosty stars that
   frozen courses run.

They talked of wise and wondrous things
    that made my spirits sing.
They made a garland from the winds and
    crowned me as a king.

They took my hand and ran with me and
    all grew hushed and still.
The rivers dwindled as we passed. We
    strode from hill to hill.

The world became a grain of sand washed
    in a mighty sea,
And time became a withered leaf blown
    from its parent tree.

The Letter

There was once a boy called James who lived with his father and grandmother in a flat in the city. His grandmother said the flat was 'convenient', and by this she meant it was close to James's father's office, close to the shops in the city's main street, and close to the school as well. Indeed the school was just across the road, but James did not find it convenient at all. All his friends lived miles away and came to school in buses, and of course this meant that they lived miles away from James too, so that in the holidays, when there was no school, he was often very lonely.

His grandmother did her best. She played snakes and ladders with him and helped him make wonderful scrapbooks. She spread newspaper out on the carpet so that he could paint, and read him all sorts of exciting stories. In spite of all this, James used to miss the company of boys, and he would feel lonely for all sorts of things he had never really done before – lonely for going barefoot, climbing trees, shouting, fighting and catching frogs. Quite a lot of people have felt like this at one time or another when they were eight years old, but James did something about it, and it happened like this.

Every now and then at dinner time Mr Wilson, James's father, would stare into space for a moment and then say, 'I wonder how Dorian Ashley is getting on these days.'

Then Mrs Wilson, James's grandmother, would look disapproving, but James would prick up his ears, waiting for his father to go on.

Mr Wilson would start dreamily, 'Do you remember one time when Dorian Ashley . . .' and then would come a story. From listening to all these 'Do you remembers . . .' James learnt enough stories about Dorian Ashley to fill a book as long as a scrapbook and many times as thick.

Dorian Ashley had been a great one for running away from places. First he had run away from school, and then he ran away from home and went to sea. Then he ran away to get married, and when he was married, he and his wife went all over the world having strange adventures. Dorian Ashley had flown aeroplanes, got shipwrecked on an island, had ridden elephants and camels. He had hunted man-eating tigers, and had worked in a circus wrestling a bear. The stories went on and on and there appeared to be no end to the things he had done.

Dorian Ashley soon seemed like some

hero, vast and shadowy, with his feet in the forests and his head blotting out the moon, striding around the world from island to island. What was most surprising of all was that this mysterious wild man wasn't just a person in an adventure book, but was actually James's uncle, and the wife he had run away with was James's aunt. They had some children too, but neither Mr nor Mrs Wilson knew very much about them, which was a pity. James used to wonder about them, for they were his cousins and he felt he wanted to know them, more than he wanted anything else in the world.

Then one day his father cleared out a forgotten box and gave James a few big envelopes, some spare paper, an old diary with blank pages for drawing in and a few other things. Looking through the diary James found an address staring up at him. It was written in big sprawling writing and it

said, 'Dorian Ashley, Hill House, Titirangi, Auckland, New Zealand.'

So that was where Uncle Dorian lived, thought James. An idea came to him. He would write a letter to his uncle and aunt and cousins and post it without telling anyone. How surprised his father and grandmother would be when he showed them the letter he would get in reply!

So that is what James did. He wrote as

carefully and neatly as he could. First he told his uncle and aunt and cousins who he was. Then he told them how well he was feeling and what class he was in at school. After this he told them how very much he would like to meet them, and what fine weather it was in Wellington at present, and then he felt he had written quite enough. After all he was only eight and found writing quite hard work. He put the letter in one of the big brown envelopes his father had given him, bought a stamp with his own money, and posted it.

James waited and waited for letters, but not one came. At first he felt all warm and excited inside and then, later, he felt sad, but no matter how he felt there was no answer at all. At last he told his father what he had done, but his father just smiled and said, 'Uncle Dorian left that place years and years ago and we haven't heard from him since. What a pity! He would have written to you if he had been there. He liked children very much and would have been pleased to get a letter from you.'

As time went by James forgot about the letter though not about his Uncle Dorian and unknown cousins. However, there was a surprise in store for him and, a year later when he was nine and it was school holidays again, the surprise happened.

There he was sitting at dinner with his grandmother and father, feeling that the holidays were going to be just a little dull and uninteresting, when there was a *click* out in the hall. Someone had opened the front door without knocking. His father and grandmother looked at each other in surprise as footsteps came swiftly towards the dining-room. Then, as they all watched, amazed, the dining-room door slowly opened, and someone James had never seen before came in.

He was a huge man so untidily dressed

that he looked like a giant scarecrow. His
hair which was copper coloured came
down almost to his collar, and his eyes
burned greenish-blue under their coppery
brows, in a face which was a deep hard
brown with sun and wind.

They all stared at one another for a
moment.

'Goodness gracious! It's Dorian!' said Mr
Wilson. He sounded delighted.

'Dorian!' said Grandmother Wilson. She sounded disapproving, but then James could see at a glance that this was the sort of uncle his grandmother would disapprove of, especially in her clean convenient house.

'What on earth are you doing here, Dorian?' she asked.

'I was invited,' said Uncle Dorian, smiling a slow warm smile.

'Not by me!' said Grandmother Wilson firmly.

Then Uncle Dorian took from his pocket a folded, crumpled, dirty brown envelope. It was crissed and crossed all over in different sorts of writing – square writing, pointed writing, writing with loops and plain writing. Different languages jostled each other from top to bottom on both sides. But the largest squarest letters were printed on the front in James's own faded printing.

'Dorian Ashley', they said. It was James's

own letter to his uncle, readdressed and restamped many times.

'James sent it to me,' Uncle Dorian said. His voice was dark and rough-sounding, as if it was a black bear speaking and not a man. 'This letter has chased me all round the world. It has gone through France, Egypt, Hong Kong, South America . . . friends of mine kept on sending it on by plane, train and by sea too. It's a widely travelled letter and I think I'll keep it forever. Funnily enough it had to come all the way back home to find me. I came to see James and to invite him to come up north with me and spend the holidays with his cousins – but since I'm here and I've got a lot of room in the car, why don't you all pack up and come? You'd all be welcome.'

And that is just what they did. Mr Wilson took a special holiday from the office and off they went to Uncle Dorian's house by the sea, and had the most exciting holiday you could imagine. James found he had five cousins, some older than he was, and some younger. One of them, however, was a boy just his own age. When the weather was fine, they taught him how to swim, how to make houses in trees and dams over the creek. When it rained James showed them how to make scrapbooks, and little dishes and animals out of clay, which they painted and baked in the oven. So everybody was happy, and learning something new. Even Grandmother Wilson forgot to look disapproving and enjoyed the sun and sand. She got quite brown.

Every holiday after that James went to stay with his cousins (for, after all his travelling, Uncle Dorian had settled down to write a book about his adventures), so James was never lonely in the holidays again.

But, mind you, this would never have happened if James hadn't written that letter which had chased Uncle Dorian round the world, reminding him at last that he had a nephew in Wellington. The letter couldn't tell of its adventures but no doubt it had had some. It certainly looked adventurous in its battered way, like an old pirate with memories of strange ports and people, and whenever it was shown to anybody the different writings and languages on it spoke to them in the voices of the world.

Bush Wedding

The parson-bird shall marry us,
The bell-bird ring the bell.
The wax-eye shall our witness be
And all will then be well.

The morpok shall provide the feast,
The kiwi bird the key
That opens doors to magic lands
Where you may come with me.

The Road
to School

One day Teddy's mother had to go out for the morning and could not take Teddy. Because of this, it was specially arranged that Teddy could go to school with his brother Gerard - but just for the morning.

So this day in spring Teddy and Gerard went off to school together. It was just ordinary for Gerry, but for Teddy it was a new strange morning and he looked out at its pale blue and gold with interest and wonder. He wore neat clothes and had a lunch of an apple, and even two sandwiches,

because his mother did not know quite
when she would be calling to collect him.

As she kissed them goodbye their mother
looked into their eyes, and saw that Teddy's
eyes were wide and brown and serious, but
that Gerry's were excited like happy blue
water, and secrets like mermaids were
swimming in them.

'Funny Gerry!' she said, hugging him.
'What are you thinking?'

Gerry just laughed and shook his head.
But as they went out through the gate,
beginning the mile walk to the school,
Gerry said to Teddy: 'Now you will meet
my friends!'

'At school?' Teddy asked.

'No, on the way there,' Gerry replied.

Well, it was spring, and the poplars were
blushing green with it, and the hills were
misty, soft and dreamy. Down where their
own road crossed the main road, a breeze
sprang up as they went by, and twirled in

the dust. The dust rose until it was Teddy-high, in a little whirling, furry grey cone, like a spinning top.

'Here's my first friend,' said Gerry. Teddy peered at the whirling dust, and just for a moment he saw a strange face look out from it, then duck back again – a little grey face with a slanting, sideways look, and he knew someone was in there who did not want to be seen.

'Gerry,' the dust said in a furry, furtive voice, 'who is that with you?'

'My brother Teddy,' Gerry said proudly. 'He's going to school with me – but just for this morning.'

'Ah, ah,' said the faraway voice. 'School is it? That's the place for learning isn't it? That's where you learn the words and the dance of them isn't it?'

'We have spelling and writing sentences,' Gerry said uncertainly.

'Well, a first day must be a special day,' the dust murmured on. 'So I will give you a gift. It's not the bigness or the brightness of it you must go by, but the way it flowers when the right words are spoken.' Then a thin arm, and a hand that was half a paw, and half a claw, snaked out, and dropped into Gerry's hand a small glass tube of sand. And then the wind died down, and the dust died down, and there was nothing at all.

'Who was that?' asked Teddy.

'I don't know his real name,' Gerry replied, 'but I call him the Little Grey Whirling Fellow, and he is made utterly all of dust.'

So they went on their way.

Yes, it was spring, and the farmhouses had put on their dancing frocks of pink and white fruit blossom, and maybe, when the people were asleep, they danced up the valley and down the valley, all wild and glad with the spring.

'Here's another friend,' Gerry said. Teddy peered up into a barberry tree and found that it wasn't a tree at all, but a man with his legs rooted into the ground, branching arms held high, green and growing, over his head. From his temples sprouted flowering barberry tree antlers. His face looked down brownly and secretly at Teddy.

'The Little Gerard!' he said. 'And who is this?'

'Teddy, my brother,' Gerry answered,

'going to school with me, but just for the morning.'

'I thought you were a tree,' Teddy remarked.

'I don't know what I am,' the tree-man said thoughtfully. 'Once I was a man, but an old brown tattooed woman bewitched me to be rooted here like a tree. I make a good tree though, and I was a poor sort of man – cruel and mean, and unhappy of course. Yet, when I found myself here, bound and branching, everything came right for me. I stretched my arms up to the sun, I pushed my roots deep into the warm, rich, brown earth, my misery flowed away and gladness came into me with the sunshine – and peace too.'

'He *likes* being a tree,' Gerry said in a pleased voice to Teddy.

'So it is your first day at school,' the tree-man went on. 'Today, once again, spring lifts my heart, and besides a first day should be a

76

special day, so I shall give you a gift.' With one twiggy, thorny hand he dropped a blue seed into Teddy's brown curled paw, and then he turned his face up to drink the sunlight.

'What is his name?' Teddy asked as they moved off down the road.

'I call him Just Barberry because that is the kind of tree he is,' Gerry replied. The boys stopped where the road passed over a culvert, and a little muddy stream flowed out under their feet. They could see their reflections in the dark velvety water. Gerry whistled.

'I have another friend,' he said.

Then almost frighteningly the smooth curtain of water tore apart, and a head covered in green, slimy waterweed, dripping wet and wild, came out. But Teddy saw at a glance that this time it was just an ordinary bog-woman such as you might find anywhere.

'Who's he?' she asked Gerry abruptly.

'He's Teddy, my brother, and he's going to school, just for this morning.'

'Ah well,' she muttered, nodding at Teddy, 'you won't like it much, but I suppose you've got to go.'

'Little Grey Whirling Fellow and Just Barberry said it was a special day and gave us presents,' Teddy remarked cunningly.

'Them!' the bog-woman exclaimed, her nostrils curling with scorn. She pulled something shining out of her hair. 'I'll give you a gift too, but just because you've got eyes the same colour as my boggy little stream here.' Gerry scrambled down the bank. 'What is it?' Teddy asked him when he got back on to the road.

'Just a bottle of water!' Gerry said. 'Never mind! We'll wait and see, because you can't be at all sure of gifts, from such in-between people as they are.'

And Gerry was right because – but the

story is bolting away too fast. Gerry's school was a small one, and there was only one teacher. There were twenty-five children of all ages from five to seven and all kinds of sizes. While the teacher taught some of them the others worked away by themselves. But you couldn't help overhearing what was going on sometimes, and Gerry (and Teddy beside him) heard the teacher telling the older children about Africa.

'It has great deserts too,' the teacher was saying, 'especially in the north.'

At that very moment there came a pop and a tinkle of glass. The tube of sand Little Grey Whirling Fellow had given them burst, and the sand ran out. But so much sand! It flowed everywhere pushing away the walls of the school house. Then the chimney turned into a date palm, and there they were – a school of children and their teacher all on their own in the desert.

'This is most gratifying!' the teacher said, in delight. 'We shall all be able to profit by this.'

Then from behind a date palm came an Arab in flowing robes and he led twenty-six camels, one as white as a moonbeam. The Arab bowed to the teacher. 'Ah! Excellent!' the teacher cried. 'And I shall have that white one!' he added.

Ah – the desert – the silent rosy morning, and the camels padding across rippled sand – the fantastic domed cities, jewelled and forbidden – the sandstorms – the cold clear nights – none of them would ever forget these things. How long were they there? Who can say! They seemed to ride for days and days. But then, suddenly came cries and the shooting of guns. Wild Arabs were upon them, riding horses as black as thunder, as red as fire. 'Quick, children, into that pyramid!' the teacher shouted. So they rode their camels into a nearby pyramid . . . and lo and behold, the camels became their desks, and the pyramid was the schoolroom.

'Well, that was very educational,' declared the teacher, shaking the sand out of his trousers. 'But I see it is only ten a.m., so I will take Group Three for spelling.'

The surprises weren't over yet, for the first word he asked them to spell was 'Jungle'. Then the blue seed heard and popped open – out came the creepers and trees, with great glossy green leaves – out came butterflies with painted, glowing wings – out came flowers as big as cupped hands, all crimson, and golden and dripping with honey. The school sprouted and grew upward, and there they were ... twenty-five children and a teacher in the jungle.

'This is very fortunate,' the teacher observed. 'Children, the jungle is all around us. Notice please that it is spelt JUNGLE. Now we shall see what we can learn.'

They seemed to be there many hot

burning days and dark, warm nights. They saw humming birds and monkeys, wild spotted leopards and herds of elephants with pale moony tusks. And at last they came to a city made entirely of ivory, so magical and strange they scarcely dared to tread its lost streets or look in its empty windows. But as they stood, half bewitched, a hundred tigers with orange-and-black striped coats, and eyes like chinky emeralds, sprang after them.

'Quick, children, in here!' the teacher called, pushing them into a black doorway, and nobly being the last man in. But twink! It was their schoolroom and only eleven a.m.

'Life is full of surprises,' the teacher remarked, mopping his brow, 'but few are as pleasant as that one. Still, we must press on. Group One, I will now hear your reading. Gerard, will you begin?' Gerard began to read.

'The new word for today is Water,' the teacher said, but as he spoke the lid of Gerard's desk flew open, the cork burst out of the bog-woman's bottle, and the water leaped up like a fountain. Indeed, less a fountain than a wave, it swept down on them, and then suddenly was sea-green. There they were . . . twenty-five children and a teacher deep under the sea, with fish like birds and butterflies around and above them, and seaweed spreading its lacy shawls before them.

'The new word, I repeat, is "Water",' the teacher said firmly. 'It is all around us at this moment.'

A mermaid came by leading a school of merry dolphins. The teacher and the children each chose a dolphin to ride, and set out to make the sea their own.

There was a wonderful adventure in a world of silence and salt. They saw whole drowned kingdoms, sunken from the land,

castles and kings and the shells of ships held
in the scaly embrace of the sea serpents.
And just as they dared to approach the
loveliest ship of all, a golden galleon
blooming with the strange flowers of the
sea, a treasure of jewels spilling from her
broken side onto the blue sand, they were
horrified to see a hundred sharks, snaky-
green and white, charging on them.

'Quick, children, into the ship!' the teacher

called, and they swam over the side and onto the deck, down her companionway – and back into the schoolroom again . . . and it was only twelve o'clock.

'A most instructive morning,' the teacher said wearily, 'but very tiring.' And when he went home for lunch, his wife was amazed to see him sandy from the desert, sunburned from the jungle, and salty from the sea.

'How did you like school?' Teddy's mother asked him later.

'Well, it was all right . . .' Teddy said. 'It was very special really!'

'It isn't always like that,' Gerry said quickly.

'It's the road to school that's best,' Teddy went on, yawning. 'Because it's ours. The desert, and the jungle, and the sea aren't ours, but Little Grey Whirling Fellow, Just Barberry and the bog-woman . . . they're ours, aren't they, Gerry?'

The Pines

Hear the rumble,
Oh, hear the crash.
The great trees tumble
The strong boughs smash.

Men with saws
Are cutting the pines –
That marched like soldiers
In straight green lines.

Seventy years
Have made them tall.
It takes ten minutes
To make them fall.

And, breaking free,
With never a care,
The pine cones leap
Through the clear, bright air.

The Boy Who Went Looking for a Friend

Once there was a little boy called Sam. He said to his mother, 'I am lonely. Where can I find a friend?'

His mother said, 'Behind our house is a field. It is filled with grass and red poppies and cornflowers. There are ears of wild wheat. There are big brown and yellow butterflies. Go into the field, Sam. Perhaps you will find a friend there.'

The little boy went into the field. Among the poppies and the grass he met a tiger. The tiger was as yellow as sunshine. Over his coat were beautiful dark stripes. He had a very long twitching tail. 'Hello, tiger,' said Sam.

'Hello, Sam,' said the tiger. He yawned a tiger yawn. His teeth looked very white.

'Are you the sort of tiger that eats boys?' asked Sam.

'No!' said the tiger. 'I only eat sandwiches. I have some sandwiches wrapped in lunch paper. Would you like some?'

Sam and the tiger had a picnic on the grass. Then they played hide and seek all over the field. They hid up trees and behind trees, and made long secret tunnels through the grass. They had a lot of fun. But at sunset the tiger said,' I must be going now.'

'Will you come back?' asked Sam.

'Perhaps I will,' said the tiger. 'Or perhaps I won't,' and off he went waving his tail.

Next day Sam said to his mother, 'I am lonely – where can I find a friend?'

His mother said, 'You know that tree

down at the bottom of our garden. It is the tallest tree in the world. Its branches are so wide that sixteen wise monkeys could dance on them and there would still be room for you. You could put a table and chairs on its branches and eat your dinner there. Go to the tall tree, little Sam. You may find friends there.'

Off went Sam to the tall tree. There on its branches danced sixteen clever monkeys.

'Hello, you monkeys!' called Sam. 'Can I climb up and dance with you?'

The monkeys made themselves into a long monkey-ladder and Sam climbed up it into the branches. On a big branch of the tree was a table and seventeen chairs. Sam and the monkeys sat down to eat. They ate pancakes and pineapple, sausages and strawberries. They drank raspberry juice out of long clear glasses. Then they all put on funny hats and laughed and sang. However, just as they were all having a lovely time the sun set. The monkeys started to climb the tree. They climbed much faster than Sam could.

'Where are you going to, monkeys?' he called.

'Higher up, higher up,' the monkeys squealed.

'Will you come back tomorrow?' asked Sam.

'Perhaps,' said the monkeys, 'or perhaps not.' Off they went, swinging by their tails.

Next day Sam said to his mother, 'I am lonely. Where can I find a friend?'

'Outside our gate,' said his mother, 'is a long road. It leads from a big town to a small town. It is dusty and grey. Along that road go all sorts of people. Some are in cars, some are on horses, some are on bicycles. Sometimes nobody goes by for a long time. But listen . . . I hear music on the road. Run and see, little Sam! It might be a friend.'

Sam heard the music and ran down to the gate.

'*Ta-ra-ra-ra!*' went the trumpet. '*Rat-a-plan-plan!*' went the drum. A circus was coming by. There were white horses and black horses. There were lions and elephants. There were packets of peanuts and popcorn and a hundred balloons. Best of all was Jimmy, the funny clown. The circus stopped.

'Here is Sam!' said Jimmy. 'Let's show him the circus.' The juggler juggled plates and

cups and balls and balloons for Sam. He did
not drop one. The elephants danced. A
lovely fairy girl rode her white horse. She
stood on its back, light as a feather, and did
not fall off once. The men on the flying
trapeze swung to and fro and tossed and
turned in the air. Sam clapped and shouted.
Most of all he laughed at Jimmy the funny
clown riding his donkey backwards. Then it
was sunset. The circus began to go on down
the road.

'Where are you going?' called Sam.

'Farther on! Farther on!' called Jimmy the
funny clown.

'Will you ever come back?' asked Sam.

'Perhaps we will, or perhaps we won't,'
said Jimmy. Off they went round a bend in
the road.

The next day Sam was too sad to ask his
mother where he could find a friend.

'All my friends go away,' he thought.
'They all go to places where I can't go.' He

went down to the river. He sat with his feet
in the watercress. Then round a bend in the
river came a little boat with a blue sail. It
came past Sam. Then it stopped by the
watercress and a boy got out. He was just
Sam's size of boy, with an ordinary brown
face and brown hair.

'Hello!' he said. 'I didn't know you lived
here. My name is Philip. What's your name?'

'Sam!' said Sam.

'Get in my boat and we will sail some more,' said Philip. They sailed all afternoon. Up and down the river bank they went, watching the fish in the clear green water. They saw wild ducks swimming and cows coming down to drink. They saw a wild, bright pheasant in the long grass. All the time they talked and made up stories. It was the best day of all. When it was sunset Philip said, 'We must go home now or our mothers will come calling us. May I come and play with you tomorrow, Sam? You are a good sort of friend to share my boat with me.'

'Of course,' said Sam, very pleased. 'We've had a good time, haven't we?'

'Tomorrow will be even better,' said Philip.

Sam went home and said to his mother, 'I've got a friend, and it isn't a tiger, and it isn't monkeys, and it isn't a circus. It's a boy called Philip.'

'That's good,' said his mother. 'Tigers are

good friends for tigers. Monkeys are good friends for monkeys, and a circus is everybody's friend, but a boy is the best friend for a boy.'

'I didn't have to ask him to come and play tomorrow. He asked *me*,' said Sam.

'He sounds the best sort of friend then,' said Sam's mother.

'He wasn't in a field or up a tree or coming down the road,' said Sam. 'I met him by the river.'

'Ah, now,' said Sam's mother, 'the river brings all things to those who wait.'

And this story is called, 'The Boy Who Went Looking for a Friend', and here is an end to it.

Clowns

Zing! goes the cymbal. Bang! Goes the
  drum.
See how they tipple-topple-tumbling come,
Dazing the country, dazzling the towns.
Here's the procession of the circus clowns.

Hop on the heel and twist on the toe.
See how they wibble-wobble-waddling go.
Bim-bam-balloons in the clear blue air!
Clowns on the march to they-don't-know-
  where.

Painted-on smiles that are long and loud
Beam at the giggle-gaggle-goggling crowd.

Under the paint do they grin so gay?
Nobody sees so I just can't say.

Look how the clowns all a-cantering come
Riding their donkeys with a hee-haw-hum.
Where have they come from? Where do
   they go?
They kin-can't say for they din-don't know.

The Witch Dog

There was once a mother whose children had all grown up and gone working or got married. This mother now had nothing to do but tidy her already tidy house and weed her neat garden. This was not so very interesting for her. So, one day, this mother – her name was Mrs Rose – said to her husband, 'I find life a bit slow just now, with the children all away. I think I'll join a club, or take a class in something.'

'That's a good idea,' said Mr Rose. 'How about playing bowls?' (He played bowls himself, you see.)

'Well, no, I don't fancy that,' said Mrs Rose.

'I'd never be good enough to play with *you*, dear. No, I've had something in mind for a day or two: I think I'll learn to be a witch. I saw in the paper that they were having classes at night school.'

'They certainly have some interesting classes at night school these days,' said Mr Rose. 'Just as you like, my dear. You will enjoy it.'

Mrs Rose turned out to be very good at witchcraft. When other pupils were struggling to pull rabbits out of hats, Mrs Rose was able to pull out ribbons, sparrows, buttercups and daisies, little silver fish, frogs, dragonflies and poems written in gold on pink paper. She found it easy. The Head Witch was pleased.

'My dear Witch Rose,' she said, 'you are doing excellently - EXCELLENTLY. You may come and dance at our Witch Dance as soon as you have mastered your broomstick technique.' Mrs Rose was delighted – it was a special honour to be allowed to dance in a witch dance, and she knew she was the only one in the class to be invited. She worked hard with her broomstick. First she learned to balance and then to soar, and soon she was soaring and swooping like a cinder in the wind.

'Well, Witch Rose,' said the Head Witch, 'you're a most creditable pupil. Next Friday you may come to our Witch Dance and

we'll be pleased to have you. You must make yourself a cloak and hat and get yourself a cat, too, if you haven't got one already.'

Mrs Rose suddenly looked very dismayed.

'A cat!' she said, but the Head Witch had whisked off hastily to talk to some other pupil not nearly as clever as Mrs Rose.

'A cat!' muttered Mrs Rose, for there was something she hadn't told the Head Witch – something she hadn't even thought about, something that meant perhaps, that she could never ever be a true witch and dance at the Witch Dances.

'How am I going to get along?' she cried to Mr Rose. 'Cat's fur makes me sneeze my head off if the cat comes close. I won't be able to go, and I would like to, having got so far. But even a kitten makes me sneeze.'

'Get a dog instead,' said Mr Rose. 'A small portable dog – one that will fit onto the end of a broomstick. I know it's not usual, but there we are – and dogs don't make you sneeze.'

'Oh, do you think a dog would do instead?' Mrs Rose said. 'I wonder . . . That's a good idea of yours, Tom. I'll think about it.' She didn't have to think long, for by a curious coincidence the first thing she saw when she went out for the milk next morning was a funny little lost dog – just the sort that could fit on the end of a broomstick. He had no collar but had a cheerful expression and Mrs Rose liked him at once. She liked his silvery grey coat, which was shaggy and hung down almost to his feet, and she liked his merry ears which stuck up straight into the air and then changed their minds and hung down at the tips.

'Would you like to be a witch dog?' Mrs Rose asked him, and he wriggled his nose in a dog-grin and wagged his tail. 'Very well,' said Mrs Rose, 'you shall be, and I will call you "Nightshade". That's a good witch name, and ought to please the witches.'

On Saturday night Mrs Rose put on her hat and cloak and tucked her wand into her belt. She climbed onto her broomstick. Nightshade hopped on behind as if he had been born to it. A moment later they were up in the air and Mrs Rose pointed her broomstick in the direction of Miller's Hill.

Already the bare place at the top of Miller's Hill was bustling and rustling with witches – lots of witches. They had lighted a huge fire and were standing around it, some with cats and some with solemn owls. When Mrs Rose and Nightshade glided down amongst them they were quiet enough, except for the usual witch noises like muttering, cackling and wicked screaming. But in the next moment there was scratching and scrambling and shouting, for at sight of Nightshade the cats put out their claws, puffed up their fur and

shot off into the shadows to climb trees.
The owls took off in a whirl of angry
feathers.

The Head Witch came furiously down at
Mrs Rose and Nightshade. 'What do you
think you are up to, Witch Rose? Really, my
dear, a witch can be wicked – but never,
never stupid! Why are you bringing a
daylight animal like a dog to our festivities?'

'Well,' said Mrs Rose, 'the fact is, cats make
me sneeze. I like cats, but they make me
sneeze terribly.' The Head Witch was silent
with amazement. Mrs Rose went on quickly,
'I'm sure Nightshade will make a splendid
witch dog. There's a lot to him, Head Witch,
and once the cats get used to him . . .'

The Head Witch was frowning and about
to interrupt, when a surprising and terrible
thing happened, and took her attention
away from Mrs Rose. A large toad, as big as
a cat, hopped, croaking furiously, into the
circle of witches. Their squeaking, squealing

and cackling stopped and they stared most long and hard at the toad. Even Mrs Rose, without any practice, could see that it was no ordinary hop-toad, but an enchanted witch.

'Goodness gracious, it's Smudge – Witch Smudge!' cried the Head Witch. 'I must see what's wrong. I'll deal with your problem later, Witch Rose, but I'm afraid it won't do.' She turned to the toad. 'Smudge, what are you doing here in that condition? You can speak freely. You are among friends. Or is it a joke?'

The toad croaked indignantly.

'What?' said the Head Witch. 'Not really! Smudge, you *are* a fool!'

She turned and spoke to the other witches. 'Witch Smudge has behaved imprudently and has been enchanted by an enchanter for a month. I must say he must be one of the old-fashioned sort of enchanters to turn her into a toad – but he certainly made a good job of it and there's nothing we can do about it. I only wish he'd turned her into a pound of sausages. She deserves it.'

A great groaning and moaning and howling burst forth from the leathery throats of the witches and rose up to the moon.

'The fact is,' the Head Witch murmured to Mrs Rose, 'Witch Smudge is one of the liveliest, wickedest witches in our group. She plays the liveliest, wickedest witch music. It's a delight to dance our circles to her tunes ... And now, she's got herself turned into a toad, the selfish creature. We've no other musician. I don't see what we are going to do.'

Upon hearing this, Mrs Rose's silvery dog, Nightshade, sat back on his hind legs and from under his long silvery coat he whipped out a little violin – a little violin made of silvery wood with three green

strings and one golden one. He snatched a
twig of golden rod, and drew it over the
strings, which played a few notes of the
maddest, gayest, wickedest witch-music that
you ever heard.

The cats slid down from their trees and
the owls came circling down out of the
night. The witches began to jig and kick,
showing their red-and-black-striped
stockings. Then Nightshade really began to

play, and oh, how those witches whirled and swirled. The owls spun and spiralled in the night air, the cats crouched and pouched and boxed each other with delight in the shadows, while the music grew faster and faster and more piercing. When at last it stopped, all the witches, owls and cats fell in a heap on the top of Miller's Hill, legs kicking out in all directions. The Head Witch disentangled herself, biting somebody's leg as she did so, and felt around among the cats and owls and the other witches until she found Mrs Rose, who was in the dance with the best of them. They shook hands warmly.

'That was no ordinary music,' said the Head Witch. 'And you are no ordinary witch, Witch Rose. You can keep your dog, and we'll give him the title of Witch-Cat Extraordinary.'

So that is why, whenever the witches meet on Miller's Hill for their wicked frolics,

Mrs Rose is always dancing among them – one of the most respected witches to come out of night school. And, playing the wild, shrill music on his fiddle, Nightshade dances too – the first dog ever to become a witch cat.

A Witch Poem

The witch my sister from over the sea
Wonderful presents has sent to me.
A whistle to blow and a bell to ring,
Silver ropes for a shining swing,
A golden lion that will play and purr,
Dancing slippers of silver fur,
And, sharp as a needle, bright as a pin,
A mouse that plays on the violin.

The Strange Egg

Once Molly found a strange leathery egg in the swamp. She put it under Mrs Warm the broody hen to hatch it out. It hatched out into a sort of dragon.

Her father said,' This is no ordinary dragon. This is a dinosaur.'

'What is a dinosaur?' asked Molly.

'Well,' said her father, 'a long time ago there were a lot of dinosaurs. They were all big lizards. Some of them were bigger than houses. They all died long ago . . . All except this one,' he added gloomily. 'I hope it is not one of the larger meat-eating lizards as then it might grow up to worry the sheep.'

The dinosaur followed Mrs Warm about. She scratched worms for it, but the dinosaur liked plants better.

'Ah,' said Molly's father. 'It is a plant-eating dinosaur – one of the milder kind. They are stupid but good-natured,' he added.

Professors of all ages came from near and far to see Molly's dinosaur. She led it around on a string. Every day she needed a longer piece of string. The dinosaur grew as big as ten elephants. It ate all the flowers in the garden and Molly's mother got cross.

'I am tired of having no garden and I am tired of making tea for all the professors,' she said. 'Let's send the dinosaur to the zoo.'

'No,' said father. 'The place wouldn't be the same without it.'

So the dinosaur stayed. Mrs Warm used to perch on it every night. She had never before hatched such a grand successful egg.

One day it began to rain ... It rained and

rained and rained and rained so heavily that the water in the river got deep and overflowed.

'A flood, a flood – we will drown,' screamed Molly's mother.

'Hush, dear,' said Molly's father. 'We will ride to a safe place on Molly's dinosaur. Whistle to him, Molly.'

Molly whistled and the dinosaur came towards her with Mrs Warm the hen, wet and miserable, on his back. Molly and her father and mother climbed onto the dinosaur's back with her. They held an umbrella over themselves and had warm drinks out of a thermos flask. Just as they left, the house was swept away by the flood.

'Well, dear, there you are,' said Molly's father. 'You see it was useful to have a dinosaur, after all. And I am now able to tell you that this is the biggest kind of dinosaur and its name is Brontosaurus.'

Molly was pleased to think her pet had such a long, dignified-sounding name. It matched him well. As they went along they rescued a lot of other people climbing trees and house tops, and floating on chicken crates and fruit boxes. They rescued cats and dogs, two horses and an elephant which was floating away from a circus. The dinosaur paddled on cheerfully. By the time they came in sight of dry land, his back was

quite crowded. On the land policemen were
getting boats ready to go looking for people,
but all the people were safe on the
dinosaur's back.

After the flood went down and
everything was as it should be, a fine medal
was given to Molly's dinosaur as most
heroic animal of the year and many
presents were given to him.

The biggest present of all was a great big

swimming-pool made of rubber so you could blow it up. It was so big it took one man nearly a year to blow it up. It was a good size for dinosaurs of the brontosaurus type. He lived in the swimming-pool after that (and Molly's mother was able to grow her flowers again). It is well known that brontosauruses like to swim and paddle. It took the weight off his feet. Mrs Warm the hen used to swim with him a bit, and it is not very often you find a swimming hen.

So you see this story has a happy ending after all, which is not easy with a pet as big as ten elephants. And just to end the story I must tell you that though Molly's dinosaur had the long name of Brontosaurus, Molly always called it 'Rosie'.

Dining Out

Out in the darkness –
Harry and me –
Having a fork-and-fingers
Tea.
Potatoes boiled
In an old black pot,
And eggs for supper –
That's what we've got.
Smouldery red,
The planet Mars
Mirrors our fire
Among the stars,
And sparks leap into

The gentle night
Like baby comets ablaze
With light.
The trees and the grass
Draw close to see –
Out in the darkness,
Harry and me.

The Great Tractor Rescue

There was once a pair of boys called Teddy and Gerard who lived in a long secret valley. Wherever they looked there were hills, dark spiky pine trees, and bright streams filled with eels and watercress. It was just the sort of valley for boys to enjoy themselves in. Each weekday they went to school, but Saturday and Sunday were all their own, and they wandered all over the valley visiting both friends and friendly places.

One of their friends was a very strange

old woman indeed. Her name was Mrs Estelle Tadworthy and she had a son who was a bank manager and lived the respectable life. Mrs Estelle Tadworthy, however, was not respectable. Everyone called her Mrs Weeds, because every weekend she left her house in the town and came out to the country to collect plants. Not garden plants either, for she scorned those. She chose the wild and weedy ones. She did not ever call them weeds, however, but always referred to them as 'herbs'. Most people thought Mrs Weeds was a little mad and she did look rather unusual wearing curious brown smocks which she wove and dyed herself, and funny old sandals tied up with string. She wouldn't wear a hat at all. Her long grey hair either tossed and tangled around her brown face or stuck out in two tight little plaits with green ribbons on the end. Rain or shine she always carried a stout green umbrella. It didn't worry her when people said she was crazy.

'Because I'm brown doesn't mean I'm dirty,' she would say. 'Because I don't do the same as every other fool, but like my own foolishness best, doesn't mean to say I'm crazy. Some like me, some don't,' said Mrs Weeds. 'That's how it is . . .'

Teddy and Gerard were two who liked her a lot. They liked her thin bony face and long gentle hands. They liked the way she roared with laughter at her own jokes, the way she wore purple clover flowers behind her ears and the way she talked to plants and trees as she went along the road. She gave the boys all sorts of leaves to eat, telling them how good they would be for them.

'This is sorrel and this is dandelion,' she said. 'Eat them both to help keep your livers clean.' The boys found the dandelion leaves hot to taste, but they liked the tangy flavour of the sorrel. Mrs Weeds said her liver was extremely clean and that was why she never got headaches or grumpy feelings. 'It's the dandelion and sorrel that does it,' she said.

One Saturday, just before Christmas, when the foxgloves were out, ringing white and purple bells on every hillside of the valley, and when the streams and boggy bits were green and yellow with watercress and kingcups, Teddy and Gerard went crawling behind a hedge pretending to escape from enemies. There was a rich earthy smell because the farmer who owned the field was ploughing it up to plant turnips. In fact, the boys went past his tractor standing alone by the gate where he had left it to go home for lunch.

'Anyhow, I could drive that tractor,' said Teddy.

'So could I,' said Gerard, 'but we haven't got time now – our enemies will catch us if we wait to try out a tractor.' They went crawling on. Then suddenly they heard a voice coming down the road. It was their friend Mrs Weeds talking aloud to a particularly fine foxglove.

'Hello, you fellow in your purple coat!' she shouted 'It's a lovely day. Why are you leaning over like that? Do you want to see who's going by or are your roots weak?'

'Shall we jump out and frighten Mrs Weeds?' asked Teddy in a whisper. Gerard thought perhaps Mrs Weeds would not like *that* at all, but while he was thinking this, someone else sprang out at Mrs Weeds from the other side of the road. Two tremendous tall fellows with guns and rope leaped out of the foxgloves and shouted.

'Hands up, Mrs Estelle Tadworthy!' (Which was Mrs Weeds' real name, you'll remember.) Mrs Weeds stopped and peered at them.

'You have the bleary-eyed look that

shows a lack of Vitamin A. The humble carrot would help you a lot,' she said sharply. 'And who might you be?' It was plain, however, that they were wicked robbers or some such.

'We are thieves and bandits,' said the uglier of the two men, pointing his gun at her. 'I am the thief and he is the bandit. We are going to kidnap you and never ever let you go until your rich son, Mr John

Tadworthy, prominent businessman and bank manager that he is, pays us £1,000 sterling.'

'I'll pound you and I'll sterling your friend,' Mrs Weeds replied, taking her umbrella in a firm grip. 'The first one that comes near me shall taste the power of my strong right arm.'

Which shows that, though people said Mrs Weeds was slightly mad, she was actually very sensible and brave as a lion. Gerard could see, however, that even brown strong Mrs Weeds couldn't fight two kidnappers with guns and a long snaky rope. Fortunately he had a plan. He whispered it to Teddy, and Teddy understood at once though it was very hard to hear, what with the defiant screams of Mrs Weeds and the yells of the robbers, who were being hit with the umbrella.

Gerard's plan was this – that Teddy should drive the farmer's tractor down the road to rescue Mrs Weeds. In the meantime, he, Gerard, the best runner in the school, would try to lead at least one of the kidnappers away so that there would be only one left for Mrs Weeds and Teddy to deal with. Once round the corner Gerard would climb up a certain tree, and it would be Teddy's job to drive the tractor and Mrs Weeds underneath that tree so that Gerard could drop down onto it from the branches like a monkey or Tarzan in the pictures. This way, said Gerard, they would have an exciting adventure and be helpful to Mrs Weeds as well.

Teddy could scarcely get at the tractor quickly enough. He made off, hidden by the hedge while Gerard crouched in the soft ploughed earth watching the battle that raged in the road. Mrs Weeds was fighting magnificently, but she was getting a bit tired. You could not expect an old woman to fight both a thief and a bandit even if she was a fine muscular old woman with a remarkably clean liver.

Teddy went straight to the farmer's tractor. Quick as a flash he tried the knobs and levers and found how to start it immediately. He steered it round and out through the gateway forgetting, in his hurry, to open the gate. Fortunately, its hinges were rusty and old and snapped easily, so Teddy was very soon grinding down the road, with the tractor in top gear, off to rescue Mrs Weeds. The only troublesome thing was the gate which was stuck across the front of the tractor.

Now when Gerard heard the tractor grating along the road and knew Teddy was coming, he wriggled out under the hedge and shouted, 'Leave Mrs Weeds alone!' He charged fiercely at the thief.

The thief was just about to pop a loop of rope over Mrs Weeds' head when Gerard butted him squarely in the stomach. 'Oof!'

said the thief and sat down hard on the road.

'I'm off to get the police,' Gerard said. 'I shall tell them who you are, and describe your pasty faces to the last miserable whisker.'

Naturally the kidnappers could not allow that.

'You look after the old woman and I'll catch the boy. We'll kidnap them both,' yelled the bandit, and set off after Gerard leaving the thief to struggle with Mrs Weeds. You could see the bandit did not know that Gerard was a splendid runner - the fastest in the school.

At this moment Teddy drove the tractor into sight, steering it straight for Mrs Weeds and the thief.

'Jump on, Mrs Weeds,' he called. 'Jump on!' And, looking up and seeing what was coming and who was driving it, Mrs Weeds thrust her knobbly right fist at the thief, in a fine upper-cut, and scooping up her umbrella from the road, skilfully ducked round the gate (which still hung in front of the tractor), and nipped up beside Teddy. The thief was rather dazed. First he had been butted by Gerard and then boxed by Mrs Weeds. But worse was in store for him. He was too bewildered to notice the gate. As he went to leap after Mrs Weeds he hit the gate and lay flattened and dusty while the tractor ground on its way.

'I shall hit his fingers with my umbrella if he tries to climb after us,' said Mrs Weeds, but the thief just lay in the dust and let them go on, steadily but not very fast.

They went round the corner. There was the tree with the bandit standing underneath it, looking into the branches that reached out over the road. There among the leaves crouched Gerard, like a monkey boy. The bandit who did not like climbing trees was trying to poke him down with a stick.

He stopped and peered through his horn-rimmed glasses in astonishment. He dodged out of the way of the sticking-out gate and tried to scramble onto the tractor to get at Teddy and Mrs Weeds. Mrs Weeds was waiting with her umbrella and he had to let go again. As the tractor passed under the tree Gerard swung down from the branches onto it. Off they went, leaving the bandit and the thief behind.

Mrs Weeds roared with delighted laughter, startling a bull in a nearby paddock.

'You're a fine couple of fellows,' she said. 'More than a match for any kidnappers. Usually I like a bit of a scrap, but I was getting out of breath, I must admit.' She slapped them on their backs. Teddy and Gerard looked proudly at each other out of the corners of their eyes. They grinned at Mrs Weeds. The tractor went rumble rumble bumble along the road. All seemed happy.

But . . . just at that moment a car roared up behind them and sitting at the wheel, his eyes narrow and fierce behind his glasses, was the bandit, while at his side, looking bruised and angry, sat the thief.

'Of course! They would have a car hidden!' cried Teddy in despair, for the car went much faster than the tractor. 'What shall we do?'

Then Mrs Weeds climbed up onto the engine of the tractor and unscrewed the petrol cap. From the wide pockets of her smock she took dandelions, sorrel, yarrow, forgetmenots, wild parsley and mint, clover, nettles and all sorts of plants, jammed them into the tank and then screwed the cap on again. Teddy, looking over his shoulder, saw the thief leaning out of the car window and trying to lassoo the tractor with the rope he had been using earlier for tying up Mrs Weeds. But at that moment the tractor gave a roar like a bull and leaped forward at the

speed of an express railway train. It was
plain that Mrs Weeds' plants had mingled
with the petrol in some mysterious way to
make a powerful mixture that the tractor
loved. Teddy steered, Gerard worked the
gears, and Mrs Weeds stood, tall and brown,
with her grey hair blowing out like a flag in
the wind they made by going so fast.

'We've left them miles behind,' said
Gerard, turning round. But no! There

behind them bumping and bowling along was the kidnappers' car, and the bandit and thief were crouched inside it white as unpleasant cheese, and obviously terrified. The lassoo the thief had thrown had first caught the tractor and then whipped itself into a knot round the car's bumper. Neither the bandit nor the thief could get out of the car and the car could not get free of the tractor, so they sped wildly along together, on and on up hill and down until they came in sight of the nearest town. The tractor dashed into the main street, and then suddenly, without warning, it slowed down, and it stopped right in front of the police station.

A policeman with a ginger moustache was standing outside. He looked first at the tractor and then peered into the car.

'My word!' he shouted. 'Here are those wicked criminals – the bandit and the thief. Catch them, catch them!' He blew on his whistle and policemen of all shapes and sizes came running from everywhere, seized the white-faced and trembling bandit, the battered and bruised thief and hurried them into prison, which was where they belonged.

So that was the end of the great tractor rescue in which Teddy and Gerard rescued their friend Mrs Weeds from kidnappers. But it was not quite the end because next weekend, Mrs Weeds came out to visit them and brought with her boxes of delightful seeds with instructions on how to grow them. They dug and planted (and Mrs Weeds dug and planted with them) and then they waited – and sure enough, two weeks later up came sage, up came parsley, marjoram, thyme, sweet basil, summer savory, dill, and all the nice garden herbs (pot herbs, as some call them) that give good rich tastes and smells to cooking. The boys' mother was delighted and the boys themselves were proud to have such good herb gardens, and looked after them carefully.

As for Mrs Weeds, she went on roaming the countryside, and when the story of the great tractor rescue got round, no kidnapper ever dared approach her as she strode on her way, her hair blowing grey and wild around her, her stout green umbrella under her arm, talking to trees and flowers as if they were the best of friends, as indeed they were.

Goodness Gracious!

Goodness gracious, fiddle dee dee!
Somebody's grandmother out at sea!

Just where the breakers begin to bound
Somebody's grandmother bobbing around.

Up on the shore the people shout,
'Give us a hand and we'll pull you out!'

'No!' says the granny. 'I'm right as rain,
And I'm going to go on till I get to Spain.'

The Tick-Tock Party

One day Timothy said to his mother, 'It is a long time since Christmas came. We haven't had a party for a long time. Will it be my birthday soon?'

'Not for another long time!' his mother said. 'We are halfway between Christmas time and birthday time.'

'Couldn't we have my birthday a bit sooner this year?' asked Timothy.

'Not really!' said his mother. 'It is best to have your birthday when it comes.'

Timothy looked around sadly. Out in the yard he saw Tick-Tock the old grey rocking horse.

'Couldn't it be Tick-Tock's birthday then?' he asked. 'Tick-Tock is so old his birthday cake would be like a bonfire with all its candles. Let it be his birthday.'

His mother thought for a while.

'Yes,' she said, 'Tick-Tock deserves a birthday. He is very old indeed. First he was Granny's rocking-horse, then he was mine. Now he is yours. His mane has come off and his tail is lost. All his fine paint is gone. He must feel very old and grey. We will have a party on Saturday to cheer him up.'

Timothy ran out into the yard to tell Tick-Tock.

'It is your birthday on Saturday, Tick-Tock,' he said. 'Isn't that exciting? Aren't you pleased?'

But Tick-Tock just looked as sad and grey as ever. Timothy was the one to be excited. Thursday went by, and then Friday. At last it was Saturday – the day of the birthday.

It was a beautiful sunny morning. Timothy
woke up and the first thing he did was to
run outside, pyjamas and all, to say 'Happy
Birthday' to Tick-Tock. He ran into the
sunny yard, and stopped in surprise. Tick-
Tock was not grey any more. He was
shining white all over.

Mother and Father laughed at Timothy's
surprise. 'This is part of my birthday present
to Tick-Tock,' Father said. 'I will give him

the rest of his present this afternoon when the white paint is quite dry.'

Timothy was very pleased to think that Tick-Tock had got a birthday present.

All morning he played in the yard. He could not keep his eyes off the shining white shape of Tick-Tock.

Just before lunch a car pulled up at the gate.

'Mummy!' called Timothy. 'Here are Granny and Grandpa!'

'We couldn't miss Tick-Tock's birthday,' Granny said. 'I have a present for him.'

Tick-Tock couldn't unwrap his present, so Timothy had to unwrap it for him. Granny had made a fine red saddle with golden tassels. Grandpa had a parcel too. At first Timothy could not think what it was. It seemed to be filled with long black hair.

'It is a new tail for Tick-Tock made of real horse hair,' said Grandpa. 'Your father will

nail it on for him – and the saddle too –
when the paint is dry.'

So now Tick-Tock had a new white coat,
a red saddle and a black tail.

Someone opened the gate. It was Aunty
Joan.

'I had to come to Tick-Tock's party,' she
said. 'Here is his present.'

Timothy unwrapped the parcel. It was
full of brown sheep's wool.

'It is from a special brown sheep I know,'
said Aunty Joan. 'It is a mane for Tick-Tock,
but I see you will have to wait before we
put it on.'

So now Tick-Tock had a fine brown
mane to toss in the wind.

'It does not match his tail,' said Timothy,
'but that is all the better.'

Then Anne, Timothy's big sister, came out
of her bedroom.

'Look,' she said, 'I have a present for Tick-
Tock too. It is a red bridle. I made it all myself.'

'Thank you,' said Timothy, because Tick-Tock was too busy thinking about his presents to say 'thank you' for himself.

'Well, this is all very well,' said Timothy's mother, 'but *my* present to Tick-Tock is waiting inside. Let's go in and look at it.'

Inside, the table was set for lunch, and in the middle of the table was a big birthday cake with more candles on it than Timothy had ever seen. Everyone laughed and talked and ate birthday cake.

It was a wonderful party. Outside Tick-Tock stood like a ghost horse, white and shining in the sunlight.

'Ah,' said Granny, 'I remember the morning when I first saw Tick-Tock. It was Christmas, and I was only a little girl then. He was the most wonderful Christmas present I had ever had. He was dapple grey in those days with a long white mane and tail.'

'Then, when I was small,' said Aunty Joan,

'Father – that's Grandpa to you Timothy – brought him down from the loft and painted him up again.'

'Aunty Joan and I used to play on him for hours at a time,' said Mother. 'We'd ride him together, or pretend he was a wild horse we were trying to catch and tame. Whenever I felt sad I would go and sit on Tick-Tock and rock and rock until I felt better.'

'And now he's mine,' said Timothy proudly.

'Quite a member of the family in fact,' said Father. 'I think the paint is dry enough now. We'll give Tick-Tock a really new look for his birthday.'

They all went out and watched Father nail on the black tail and track on the brown mane. He fitted the saddle and bridle on and fastened them with little nails. Last of all he took a pot of blue paint, and with a small paintbrush he painted two beautiful blue eyes for Tick-Tock to see with.

'Good old Tick-Tock,' said Anne. 'He looks like new.'

'He's smiling at me,' Timothy cried.

'So he should be, with all those presents,' said Father, laughing. He lifted Timothy onto the new red saddle. 'You give him a birthday present now, Timothy,' Father said. 'Take him for a good rocky ride.'

So Timothy rocked away, and Tick-Tock's rockers went 'Tick-Tock!' on the concrete which was, no doubt, his rocking horse way of saying 'thank you'.

Uncle James

My Uncle James
Was a terrible man.
He cooked his wife
In the frying pan.

'She's far too tender
To bake or boil!'
He cooked her up
In peanut oil.

But some time later –
A month or more –
There came a knock
On my uncle's door.

A great green devil
Was standing there.
He caught my uncle
By the hair.

'Are you the uncle
That cooked his wife,
And leads such a terribly
Wicked life?'

My uncle yowled
Like an old tom cat,
But the devil took him,
For all of that.

Oh, take a tip
From my Uncle James!
Don't throw stones
And don't call names.

Just be as good
As ever you can -

And never cook aunts
In a frying pan!

The Thief and the Magic

There was once a grubby little hut in a wood, and here lived a thief with his mother who had once been a thief too. However, she got stiffness in the joints and creaked so much that it woke up everyone in the houses she was stealing from. Because of this she went into retirement, but she missed the old days. She used to grumble at her son.

'When I was young thieves were *thieves* - real craftsmen. We worked day and night at our stealing. But nowadays young thieves only think of the money. We were above that. We'd steal *anything*, just for the love of it.'

'Yes, ma,' her young thief would say with a yawn. But mind you, this thief was very lazy, and when his mother told him to go out and steal, he'd always make some excuse and stay home in bed.

One day the thief's mother came into the room and said, 'We've run out of butter and cheese and money. Hadn't you better do some stealing?'

'Can't we eat turnips instead?' the thief asked, but his mother was determined. The thief knew he'd have to get up and steal something. Also, he was quite a kind hearted thief and hated to disappoint his old creaking mother.

'I won't have to go far,' he said. 'There's that cabin over the hill. Someone's living there now, and no doubt they will have some cheese and butter and money.'

The path over the hill was shining and
the hill itself was all golden green in the
early summer sun. If the thief had been a
poet he could have written a poem, but as it
was, his head was full of plans for stealing.
He hid behind a tree and watched the cabin.
The someone who lived there was a
raggedy little man. The thief saw him brush
his teeth, then clean his boots, and then the
raggedy man went out, walking like a

shadow right past the tree where the thief was hiding. Then the thief came out and went down to the cottage. The door was not locked – actually it was wide open. Either the little ragged man was too poor to be scared of robbers, or he had a trusting nature. The thief, stealing-bag in hand, looked around the cabin. It was very bare. There were a mop and a broom and a pair of gumboots behind the door and, hanging from nails in the wall, two long scarves – two *very* long scarves, in fact – one blue and one red. There were two boxes and a suitcase. This was all the furniture in the room. The thief opened his stealing-bag, and began stealing. He stole a nutmeg grater and a fish slice. He stole bread and cheese and jam too. He stole a calendar because he liked the picture on it.

Then he got a surprise. Something moved in the corner of the room – sat up and scratched itself. The thief had thought it was a sack, old and unravelling, but it was a dog. It looked more like a tattered sack than a dog, however, so it wasn't the thief's fault he had not realized. The dog finished scratching and lay down again, watching the thief with sharp black eyes.

'Good dog,' said the thief, but it took all the fun out of his stealing to know someone was watching him. He took a candle in a halfhearted way, put it in his bag, and made for the door.

Then something strange happened. Music began to come into the air – twangling, out-of-tune-sounding music. It rose and fell, chased itself, lost its place and went wandering. Out from behind the door came the mop and the broom dancing a solemn and stiff little dance, bowing and shaking their hair. '*Ting-tang-tong*' went the twangling music and the mop and broom began to dance in a circle round the thief. The gumboots began to shuffle and then to stamp and then to do a kicking Russian dance in the corner. The thief watched the boots uneasily for a moment. Then he looked back to the mop and the broom. Somehow they had unhooked the two scarves and were doing a scarf dance, swaying and twisting, winding in and out of their own scarves and out of each other too. The scarves made red-and-blue loops and waves and coils in the shadows of the little hut.

'Ahem,' said the thief, clutching his stealing-bag to his chest. 'Thank you I'm sure.' He wanted to please the mop and broom but he couldn't clap then because his hands were full of stealing-bag. He bowed instead, as they pirouetted on their single legs, and then he made for the open door. Then the dog sat up. All at once the mop and broom made a little rush at him. They looped the scarves round and round him until he was more like a blue-and-red

cocoon than a man. When he was bound
hand and foot and could move no more,
they bowed back to him and went to their
places behind the door, where they leaned
themselves against the door, stiff and still.
From its corner the dog watched him
keenly.

The thief lay and blinked. There was
nothing he could do about anything. At
least, since the scarves were made of wool,

he was very warm, but he could not escape.

After a while there was the sound of rustling feet and the raggedy little man came in at the door. The dog got up and went to meet him, wagging its tail.

'Oh,' said the little ragged man in surprise. 'A thief.' He went down on his knees and began to unknot and unwind the scarves.

'Yes, sir!' said the thief sharply, as soon as he could. 'I am a respectable thief, and let me tell you, this is not what I am used to!'

'I'm very sorry,' said the raggedy man humbly.

'If I had known you were a magician,' the thief went on, 'I wouldn't have come here.'

'But I'm not a magician,' said the raggedy man. 'I'm just a tramp called Jumping Bean. It's my dog who is a magician.' The dog smiled at the thief and wagged its tail as if it was a wand. 'Is this yours?' Jumping Bean asked, picking up the stealing-bag.

'Yes,' said the thief. He added sulkily, 'I suppose you'll want your things back again.'

Jumping Bean peered into the bag. 'Only the fish slice,' he said. 'Not the other things, and we don't use the nutmeg grater. We don't like nutmeg.'

The thief was now free.

'Well,' he said, 'I must say, magician or not, I'd never wish to steal from the house of a finer fellow than yourself. You've been fair – very fair, and I don't mind giving you back your fish slice.'

'Ah well,' said Jumping Bean, 'I like to help a fellow creature on his way.'

So with these words of mutual esteem the thief and the tramp parted. The thief went home to his creaking mother to boast of his stealing. But Jumping Bean and his dog sat down to eat a fine roast duck with orange sauce which the dog magicked up, because, let me tell you, that dog was a *real* magician!

Alone in the House

Who? Who? Who was that whispered?
Who was it spoke in a magical tongue?
Did some white witch pass under my
    window?
Was that a thread of the song she sung?

Dark, dark, dark grow the shadows.
Is that the rattling of goblin drums?
Alone in the house with the cat and the
    mouse,
And nobody, nobody comes.

Green Needles

All round Teddy's house marched the pine trees – more than a hundred of them. Although they were so tall, and Teddy was so small, they often nodded to each other, and Teddy felt very friendly towards them. He liked their grey, wrinkled skins and arms full of cones. He enjoyed the music the wind made in them, roaring like the sea.

One night, one of the trees fell with a crash like thunder and the end of the world. Now Teddy had a wonderful new playground as he climbed up and down and round about the fallen giant. He rode the springy branches as if they were wild, tossing horses and then slid down into pine-scented shadows below. The tree became Teddy's house, all little green rooms and passages.

Then one day while he was playing in his house he pushed through a curtain of needles and found himself in a room he had never seen before. Someone else was there before him.

'Hello!' said Teddy.

'Hello!' said the someone else.

They liked each other straight away. The someone else had greyish hair, and a brown, crinkled-up face. He wore a jacket and trousers made out of pine needles, and his eyes were green too, as green and sharp as the pine needles themselves.

'Are you a pine-tree man?' asked Teddy.

'Well, I live here at present,' the man answered. 'It suits me because my name actually is Green Needles and we match,

this tree and I. I am hiding from someone, so I have to match the place I hide in.'

'Who are you hiding from?' Teddy asked.

'A very rich, powerful queen!' Green Needles said. 'She is a bit too rich really. I did some work for her once and she wanted to keep me. But no one can keep me forever, because I don't care to be kept. Mine is a wild, free nature.'

'What was the work you did?' Teddy wondered.

'It was sewing,' Green Needles replied. Teddy thought he must mean 'sowing' like sowing seeds in a garden, but Green Needles said he meant sewing with stitches and a needle.

'I can thread a needle with sunshine and sew gold, or with moonlight and sew silver. I can make my stitches with moss, or cobwebs, with the dust on fern fronds and the feathers of a kingfisher,' boasted Green Needles, 'but I must be free. So will you let me sit here in this green room and hide, until I am quite sure it is safe for me to go out in the world again? Sooner or later they will come and search for me here, and if they don't find me they will go away and never come back. I will be safe then. Will you hide me?'

'Of course I will,' Teddy agreed, wondering who would come looking for Green Needles, 'and I will visit you sometimes.'

So that was what happened, and for several weeks Green Needles sat in his pine-tree room, while Teddy visited him and told him about the world. Then one day Teddy's mother said to him, 'I am going to visit Mrs Shaw and I'm taking the babies. Can you be a good boy and look after the house while I am away? I won't be long.' And off she went.

Teddy sat in the kitchen eating a bread slice with dates on it when the door opened. It wasn't his mother at all. It was three strange people with long, solemn faces. One was a soldier, tall and glittering in armour like fish scales. His black hair was braided with red ribbon, and in his hand he carried a long, slender spear. At his side swung a sword in a golden sheath. The second of the visitors was a woman tall and strong as a man, wearing a helmet crested with plumes and a cloak of tiger skin over her armour. Her hair, bright as a flame, fell

down over the cloak to her waist and
twisted in it were chains of silver, and of
roses. On her shoulder sat the third person,
a little old, old man, so old he had shrunken
back to child size. He was quite white. There
was white in his clothes, in his face and in
his hair. Only his eyes were black, and in his
hand he clasped a little black wand, which
he pointed at Teddy.

'You!' he cried. 'You, little boy! My wand

tells me Green Needles has been here. Where is he?'

'He isn't here,' Teddy answered quite truthfully, because Green Needles was nowhere near the house.

'A queen wants him,' the old, old man went on, 'a powerful queen. She will give you boxes of pearls and yards of crimson silk, she will give you the furs of wild white foxes. Where is Green Needles?'

'I don't know!' Teddy shook his head, and this time it was a little lie, because he knew quite well Green Needles was sitting out in his secret piny room.

'The queen will give more,' declared the old man frowning at Teddy. 'She will give fifteen baskets of scarlet roses and a musical box that sings like a blackbird. She will give a casket of silver lined with black velvet, holding a perfect diamond, and a casket of gold holding a single dew drop, also a singing cricket in a cage of ivory.'

'I would like a cricket,' Teddy said, 'but I don't know where Green Needles is.'

'Lastly,' said the old man, looking furious, 'the queen will give to the boy who tells her where Green Needles is – a chair of gold by her own chair at the table. That boy will walk beside her in the great parades, or ride beside her on a pony white as snow, or sit beside her in her coach on a seat of midnight blue velvet, and be in all ways like a son to her.'

'Well,' Teddy shook his head, 'I don't know at all where Green Needles is.'

'My wand tells me you are lying,' the old man said.

'Your wand needs fixing,' Teddy said firmly in answer. Then the old man said angrily to his friends, 'Search the house!'

They pushed past Teddy and marched into the kitchen. They pulled open the cupboards and flung the saucepans and the papers, the knives, the forks, the Marmite, the butter and the good wholesome bread onto the floor. The soldier even poked the bag puddings with his spear. They went through the house, slashing and searching. They tore books and the sitting-room carpet. The huge woman pulled the curtains down, and tugged the drawers out of the desk. The soldier ripped the blankets off the beds, and sliced the mattresses in two. Oh, it was dreadful to see how they searched – how they slit and split, chipped and chopped, hashed and gashed, wrenched, splintered, carved and quartered, and tore to tatters the poor, old house. But they could not find Green Needles.

Then they went round and round the house, and even searched the pine tree, but they did not find Green Needles in his little secret room in the pine tree's heart. So at last they stopped.

'He isn't here!' said the large woman. 'The magician's wand is wrong.'

'My wand has never been wrong before,' the old magician replied sulkily.

'This time it is wrong,' the soldier grunted heavily, 'or else Green Needles has a stronger magic than you.'

'That miserable stitcher has no magic at all!' screamed the enraged magician. None of them took any notice of Teddy who was standing near by listening.

'Then your wand is wrong,' the soldier sighed, 'and we are wasting our time. Let us go and search some other world.'

And they went off down the road, leaving Teddy to explain about the ruined house to his mother who was just coming down the hill.

Teddy's mother was not at all pleased. She could not be cross with Teddy for so nobly and bravely helping his friend, Green Needles, but it was plain she wanted to be.

'Look at the place!' she cried, over and over again. 'Just look at it! What will your father say? He's bringing visitors home this evening, too. Look, they've even emptied out the vases. Oh, and the *inkwell*! They can't have thought your friend was hiding there.'

But at that moment who should come in but Green Needles himself.

Teddy was amazed.

'You must hide!' he told Green Needles. 'People are looking for you.'

'Actually,' Green Needles answered calmly, 'I don't think they will come back. And so I can go on with my wanderings. I feel free again.'

'I thought they would find you,' Teddy said.

'Ah, but I sewed myself safely into the pine-tree room and they went by me a thousand times, not guessing I was there. So you see I am safe, and soon I will be on my way. But first, madam,' with a bow to Teddy's mother, 'I must help you.'

'What can you do?' Teddy's mother asked, looking at the wreckage.

'Madam, I can sew!' said Green Needles. And he turned back his coat collar to show a row of green needles, some as thick as a big darning needle, others as fine as the feeler of an ant. From his pocket he took silks as many-coloured as summer time.

Yes, Green Needles could sew like nobody ever sewed before. He sewed up the tears in the wall with butterflies and birds. He sewed up the tears in the carpet and, where his needle flashed, primroses appeared, with hyacinths, jonquils, crocuses and the starry yarrow – all so real they seemed to nod in the wind. Teddy's mother didn't have a carpet any more. She had a garden in every room, a garden you could walk over without bruising leaf or flower. The silks Green Needles sewed with smelled of rosemary and lavender and of pine trees.

Where the curtains had been slashed, Green Needles mended them. Some he sewed with ivy, and among the leaves he put birds' nests with blue eggs in them. Thrushes and blackbirds peeped out into the room. Other curtains he sewed with spiders' webs, fine and silken, and with dragonflies and flag irises. He sewed the chairs with a mellow thread that looked like the rich shine in fine, polished wood.

Then he looked at the ceiling where the soldier's spear had poked and scarred.

'Now I shall thread my needle with sunshine,' said Green Needles. He embroidered a laughing, jolly sun, and a silver secret moon in the centre of the ceiling, and round the edge he put the stars dancing in their beautiful patterns ... the Ram, the Twins, Taurus the Bull, Capricorn the Goat, striding Orion and the shy Seven Sisters – all the starry people shone over Teddy's head.

Then he sewed up the mattresses with stitches like a procession of ladybirds. Even the pages of the books he stitched together with tiny white and black threads, so that you couldn't tell where they had been torn. Oh, Green Needles, Green Needles, there was never another like you – you were the greatest stitcher in the world.

Then Green Needles put his needles back in his coat collar, and his silks back in his pocket.

'Now I can be on my way,' he said, 'for they won't come here any more. They won't dare to admit I was hiding all the time and they missed me. If you knew what their queen was like, you would understand. A handsome woman, mind you, but sharp in the temper. They've gone off to search for me among the stars.'

'Are you sure you won't stay a little longer?' asked Teddy's mother. 'Stay for tea!'

'I don't think so,' said Green Needles. 'My

inside tells me I need space and sunshine, the open road and trees and flowers, stars and seas. In short, I need some wandering. The world gives me its colours, and its shapes and its shadows, and they all come out in my sewing. That is how I give them back to the world.'

So they thanked him and off he went, and Teddy never saw him again in all the world. But the flowery carpets, the sun and the stars on the ceiling, the butterflies and kingfishers on the walls – these remained as if the outside world had come into Teddy's house to keep him company, and liked it so much it had decided to stay there. So after that, because he had helped Green Needles, Teddy walked sweet and saw gay, inside as well as out, for almost forever.

Christmas
in New Zealand

Our Christmas Day is blue and gold
And warm our Christmas night.
Blue for the colour of Mary's cloak
Soft in the candlelight.
Gold for the glow of the Christmas star
That shone serene and bright.
Warm for the love of the little babe
Safe in the oxen stall.
We know our Christmas by these signs
And yet around my wall
On Christmas cards the holly gleams

And snowflakes coldly fall,
And robins I have never seen
Pipe out a Christmas call.

Once Upon an Evening

Once upon an evening
    Looking overhead,
I saw the little crescent moon
    Like a silver thread.

Then rocks burst into blossom,
    And horns blew, sweet and shrill,
    And kings and queens in scarlet
Came shining down the hill.

When the King
Rides By

Oh, what a fuss when the king rides by
And the drum plays *rat-a-plan-plan!*

Oh, what a fuss when the king rides by –
The pusscat runs and the pigeons fly
And the drum plays *rat-a-plan-plan!*

Oh, what a fuss when the king rides by –
The dogs all bark and the babies cry,
The pusscat runs and the pigeons fly,
And the drum plays *rat-a-plan-plan!*

Oh, what a fuss when the king rides by –
The soldiers stamp and the ladies sigh,
The dogs all bark and the babies cry,
The pusscat runs and the pigeons fly,
And the drum goes *rat-a-plan-plan!*

Oh, what a fuss when the king rides by –
The people throw their hats up high,
The soldiers stamp and the ladies sigh,
The dogs all bark, and the babies cry,
The pusscat runs and the pigeons fly,
And the drum goes *rat-a-plan-plan!*

Oh, what a fuss when the king rides by –
Mice in their mousehole wonder why
The people throw their hats up high,
The soldiers stamp and the ladies sigh,
The dogs all bark and the babies cry,
The pusscat runs and the pigeons fly,
And the drum goes *rat-a-plan-plan!*

Oh, what a fuss when the king rides by –
Rockets dance in the starry sky,

Mice in their mousehole wonder why
The people throw their hats up high,
The soldiers stamp and the ladies sigh,
The dogs all bark and the babies cry,
The pusscat runs and the pigeons fly,
And the drum goes *rat-a-plan-plan!*